DATE DUE		
SEP 0 9 2007	JUN 2007	
OCT 2 2 2007		

this is my faith

Christianity

by Holly Wallace

First edition for the United States, its territories and dependencies, Canada, and the Philippine Republic published in 2006 by Barron's Educational Series, Inc.

© Copyright 2006 by ticktock Entertainment Ltd.

First published in Great Britain in 2006 by ticktock Media Ltd., Unit 2, Orchard Business Centre, North Farm Road, Tunbridge Wells, Kent, TN2 3XF

All inquiries should be addressed to:
Barron's Educational Series, Inc.
250 Wireless Boulevard
Hauppauge, NY 11788
www.barronseduc.com

ISBN-13: 978-0-7641-5963-3 (Hardcover)
ISBN-10: 0-7641-5963-1 (Hardcover)

ISBN-13: 978-0-7641-3473-9 (Paperback)
ISBN-10: 0-7641-3473-6 (Paperback)

Library of Congress Control Number: 2005939035

Picture credits
t = top, b = bottom, c = center, l = left, r = right,
OFC = outside front cover, OBC = outside back cover

Alamy: 13b, 18b, 27t, 27c. Art Directors & Trip Photo Library: 9t, 19c, 23t, 23c. Corbis: 7b, 9c, 9b, 11t, 15b, 21c, 23b, 25t, 27b, 29t. Plan UK and Plan International: OFC, 1, 2, 4, 5t, 5c, 6all, 7c, 10all, 14all, 16all, 18t, 20t, 22t, 24, 26t, 30t, OBC. Shutterstock: 8, 12, 15c, 17t, 25c, 25b, 26b, 31tl. Superstock: 28b. World Religions PL/ Christine Osborne: (Paul Gapper: 5b) (Mimi Forsyth: 7t, 11b) 11c, 15t, 17c, 17b, 19b, 20b, 21t, 21b, 29b, 31t.

Every effort has been made to trace the copyright holders, and we apologize in advance for any unintentional omissions. We would be pleased to insert the appropriate acknowledgments in any subsequent edition of this book.

Printed in China
9 8 7 6 5 4 3 2 1

Contents

Words that appear in **bold** are explained in the glossary.

I am a Christian

"My name is Herbert and I am 11 years old. I live in Uganda, in East Africa. My family follows the religion of **Christianity**. We are **Christians**."

"My Christian faith teaches me to love God and to believe in **Jesus Christ**, the Son of God."

Herbert's Christian faith is very important in his life. He belongs to the **Pentecostal Church**.

Herbert lives in this house with his mother, three sisters, and two brothers.

"Being a Christian also teaches me how to live my life. I try to respect other people and to help those in need."

"The place where we worship is a **church**. Many churches have a cross on top or outside. The cross is a **symbol** of Jesus Christ."

A wooden cross sits on top of the tin roof of Herbert's local church.

Followers of Jesus would scratch a fish on rocks or walls as a signal to others about a future meeting. The fish is still used today as a symbol of Christianity.

"Early Christians were often **persecuted** and had to keep their beliefs and meetings secret. So they used the fish symbol like a secret password."

My family

"I live with my mother, three sisters, and two brothers. My father died a few years ago."

"Like other children, I enjoy playing with my friends. But I also try to be a good Christian. This means helping around the house and being polite and kind."

This is me, Herbert.

This is my brother, Geoffrey.

Justine, my oldest sister.

My mother, Aidah.

This is my mother's best friend.

Damalie, my middle sister.

Mary, my baby sister.

In some countries the family holds hands around the table to say grace before a meal.

"Before a meal, we say a short **prayer** called grace to thank God for the food that we are about to eat."

"My family says our prayers together several times a day to stay close to God. We bow our heads and put our hands together to show respect for him."

Before prayers, Herbert's family reads the Bible together.

Monks and **nuns** spend their lives helping others. Nuns often work with poor or sick people.

"Helping each other is an important Christian teaching. My family and I try to help our neighbors if they have any problems."

7

LEARN MORE: What is Christianity?

- Christianity began about 2,000 years ago in Palestine in the Middle East. It began with Jesus, whom Christians believe was the Son of God. Today, there are more than 2 billion Christians living all over the world.

- There are lots of different groups of Christians. The main ones are the **Roman Catholics**, **Orthodox**, and **Protestants.**

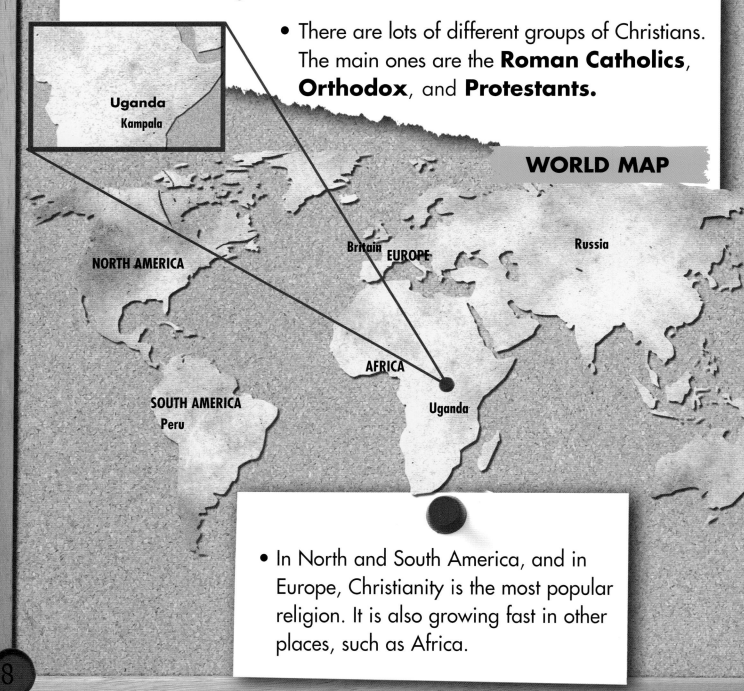

Uganda
Kampala

WORLD MAP

NORTH AMERICA

Britain EUROPE

Russia

AFRICA

SOUTH AMERICA
Peru

Uganda

- In North and South America, and in Europe, Christianity is the most popular religion. It is also growing fast in other places, such as Africa.

- These Christians in Peru belong to the Roman Catholic Church. Spanish explorers took Christianity to South America with them hundreds of years ago.

During Holy Week in Peru, images of the **Virgin Mary** and **Saint John** are carried in special parades and the streets are covered in flower petals.

This icon of the Virgin Mary and Jesus is in the Church of the Nativity in Bethlehem.

- Most Russian Christians belong to the Orthodox Church. Churches are decorated with special pictures called **icons** that show Jesus, Mary, or one of the **saints**.

A Communion service in an Anglican Church. The priest is saying a blessing over the bread and the wine.

- There are many different groups in the Protestant Church. The Anglican Church, which is also known as the Church of England, is the largest Protestant group in Britain. In the United States, the main group is the **Episcopal Church**. Pentecostal Christians, like Herbert, are Protestants too.

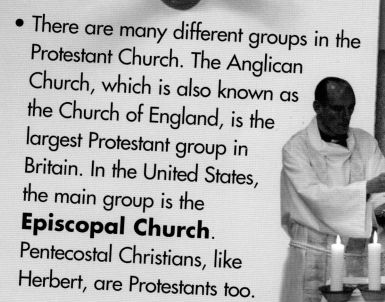

What I believe

"Christians believe that God made the world and looks after everything in it. We think God is like a father who cares for us as his children."

"We believe that Jesus came to Earth to save us from our **sins** and to show us God's love. Jesus is special because after he died, God brought him back to life again. This gives us hope that if we follow Jesus we could live with God forever, even after we die."

Like other Christians, Herbert believes the Bible contains the word of God, and teaches him how God wants him to live.

This stained glass window shows the Good Samaritan who stopped to help a man who was in trouble when others had passed him by.

"I enjoy reading the **parables**, or stories, that Jesus told when he was teaching. One of my favorites is about the Good Samaritan."

"I believe that it is important to pray to God and to Jesus. I ask them to look after me and my family and to help me be good."

Most Christians kneel when they pray. This is a sign of respect for God.

St. Francis of Assisi was an Italian monk who loved animals, especially birds. St. Francis also cared for the sick and needy.

"Some Christians pray to saints. Saints are people who have lived especially good lives and were very close to God when they were alive."

LEARN MORE: A special book

• The Bible is a holy book for Christians. It teaches them about what God is like and it tells them about Jesus's life.

• The Bible has two parts, the Old Testament and the New Testament. The Old Testament was written many years before Jesus was born and is a history of the **Jews.**

• The New Testament was written after the death of Jesus. It is about the life and teachings of Jesus.

The parable of the lost sheep tells us that God cares as much for one person who sins as all the other Christians who are good.

- The Bible contains lots of stories called **parables**. These are stories that Jesus told to teach people about God's love for them. One parable is about a shepherd who cared so much for his animals that he spent a long time searching for one lost sheep even though he had many others.

- Before books were printed they were written out by hand. The Bible was written by monks. It was also illustrated with beautiful color pictures.

This very old Bible with pictures is called an Illuminated Bible.

- Every Christian church has a pulpit. This is a raised platform where the **minister** stands to talk to worshippers about the Bible.

In some churches the Bible is kept on a special stand called a lectern. Some lecterns are in the shape of an eagle. This is to show that the Word of God is being carried into the world.

Where I worship

"I go to a church called St. Paul's Church that is in my village. I try to go twice a week. When I go to church, I wear my best clothes and speak quietly and respectfully."

"Nearly everyone in my village goes to the same church. Being together helps us to feel part of our Christian faith."

Herbert's local church is a place for people to meet as well as to pray.

Sunday School is where children learn more about the Bible after the Sunday service.

"I also go to **Sunday School**. I learn Christian songs, prayers, and Bible readings in our local language, which is called Lugandan."

"The most important part of many churches is the **altar**. It is like a special, raised table. It has a cross on it and sometimes flowers and candles, too."

Some altars have a picture or statue of Jesus. People face the altar when they pray.

The minister gives his or her sermon from a pulpit. The sermon is usually based on a story from the Bible.

"A minister leads the service in the church. During the service he or she gives a talk, called a **sermon**, about what Jesus's teachings mean."

15

How I worship

"When I go to a service in my church, we sing **hymns**, say prayers, and listen to the sermon. Some people also go up and read passages from the Bible."

"We always go to church on a Sunday. This is the special day of worship for Christians. We remember that Jesus rose from the dead on a Sunday."

On Sundays, Herbert and his family often sit with their minister and read the Bible.

People can pray anywhere at any time as God is everywhere.

"At the end of a prayer, we say 'Amen.' This means 'Let it be so.' It is a way of showing that we agree with the words of the prayer we have just said."

"Mary was the mother of Jesus. Catholics honor Mary as the Holy Mother and pray to her."

This is a stained glass window showing Mary and the baby Jesus.

At the Holy Communion service Christians remember that Jesus died on the cross for them.

"Many Christians celebrate **Holy Communion.** This is when they share a small piece of bread and some wine that have been blessed by a priest."

17

Joining the church

"When a person joins the Christian Church, a special ceremony called **baptism** takes place. It shows that a person is starting a new life with Jesus. In my church we are baptized between seven and ten years old."

"When I was baptized, I promised to believe in Jesus and to follow his teachings. It was a very happy day for me and my family."

In many African countries people are baptized in a river as Jesus was.

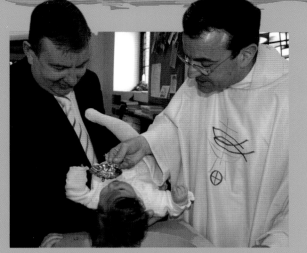

A baby is held over the **font** as the priest pours water on the baby's forehead.

"In some churches, people are baptized when they are babies. The shape of a cross is made in water on the baby's forehead."

"Many Christians are **Confirmed** in their early teens. This is when we strengthen our promises to follow the teachings of Jesus."

In some Christian churches Confirmation marks the change from being a child to being an adult.

Young Roman Catholic girls wear white dresses to celebrate First Communion.

"In the Roman Catholic Church, Christians receive their Holy Communion when they are much younger. Once they have received Communion, they can then prepare for Confirmation."

19

The life of Jesus

"Jesus was born in the town of Bethlehem, near Jerusalem. The Bible says Jesus was born in a stable because there were no rooms left in the town."

"His earthly father was thought to be Joseph, who was a carpenter. When he was young, Jesus and his family lived in Nazareth."

This is the spot where people believe Jesus was born. It is inside the Church of the Nativity in Bethlehem.

Jesus chose twelve men to be his **disciples** or special helpers. Some of them were fishermen who had boats on Lake Galilee.

"When Jesus was about 30 years old, he began teaching people about God. The religious leaders did not like what he was saying."

"The leaders of the Jewish people and the Romans, who ruled them, arrested Jesus. They put him in prison for saying he was the Son of God. Soon after he was **crucified.**"

Before Jesus was put on the cross, the Roman soldiers put a crown of thorns on his head.

Christians believe that Jesus rose from the dead on the third day after his crucifixion.

"Jesus was buried, but on the third day he came back to life. This is called the **resurrection.**"

Christmas

"For me, the happiest time of the year is Christmas. This is when we celebrate the birth of Jesus. On Christmas Day, I go to church with my family for a special Christmas service."

"We thank God for sending Jesus and remember the Christmas message of peace on Earth and goodwill to everyone."

A child lights candles during a service on Christmas Day. They mark the coming of the light (Jesus) into the world.

Many churches have a Christmas **crib** which shows the baby Jesus, Mary, and Joseph in the stable at Bethlehem.

"After church we invite our friends and relations to our house to eat with us. We have a special meal of rice and meat."

"Many children dress up and act out the story of Jesus's birth with **nativity** plays in churches and at school."

Nativity plays tell the story of Jesus's birth in the stable with Mary and Joseph, and how shepherds and wise men came to visit them.

One of the most popular Christmas services is when carols are sung by candlelight.

"Carols are special songs that are sung at Christmastime. These tell the Christmas story and thank God for sending Jesus to Earth."

23

Easter

"Easter is our most important Christian festival. This is when we remember how Jesus died and came back to life again."

"The last week of Jesus's life is called **Holy Week**. On **Good Friday** we remember the crucifixion. Then Easter Sunday is a happy day, when Jesus came back to life. We believe this shows that after we die we can start a new life with God."

Villagers in Uganda carry palm leaves on Palm Sunday to mark the beginning of Holy Week.

We call this day Good Friday because, by dying on the cross, Jesus showed his love for us.

"On Good Friday Jesus was beaten and whipped, before being nailed to a cross and left to die."

"On Easter Saturday, or Holy Saturday, a special candle is lit in some churches. It is called the **Paschal candle.**"

The Paschal candle is lit to mark the light of Christ. Other candles in church are lit from this candle.

Christians say that an egg symbolizes the resurrection because new life breaks out of its shell.

"At Easter, some Christians give each other Easter eggs. This reminds them of Jesus's new life and the hope of new life for all who follow him."

25

Special occasions

"There are many other special times in a Christian's life. When there is a wedding in my village, it is a very happy time."

"Couples often get married in church. In the wedding service they promise to love each other until they die."

During a wedding service couples usually give each other a ring, as a symbol of their love and the promises they make.

A church wedding in South Africa. Many brides wear white and have young family members as bridesmaids.

"We sing songs for the couple and pray for them to be happy and blessed. After the ceremony there is a special meal and dancing and singing."

"The Harvest Festival service reminds Christians of all the good things God has given them over the year. After the service the food is usually given to people in need."

Many churches are decorated with flowers, baskets of fruit, vegetables, and other foods.

Sometimes Christians are buried in the ground. A stone is put up to mark the grave.

"When a Christian dies, a funeral service is held. We believe that after people die, they start a new life with God."

27

LEARN MORE: *Holy places*

- There are many places in the world that are special for Christians. Where Jesus was born in Bethlehem, where he grew up in Nazareth, and where he was buried in Jerusalem are the most special of all. There are now churches in all these places and thousands of **pilgrims** visit them every year.

- Lourdes is in southwest France. It is a place of pilgrimage, where thousands of sick people go believing that they will be healed.

In 1858, a young girl called Bernadette Soubirous said she had seen the Virgin Mary in the Grotto (or cave) of Massabielle. This picture shows the grotto, where the water is believed to heal the sick.

St. Peter's Square in Rome. St. Peter's Church is one of the most important Christian churches. It contains the tomb of St. Peter, one of Jesus's closest friends and disciples.

- The most holy place for Roman Catholics is the Vatican in Rome in Italy. This is where the Pope lives. The Pope is the head of the Roman Catholic Church.

- The Church of the Holy Sepulchre is a Christian church in Jerusalem. The church is believed to mark the place where Jesus was crucified and also the tomb in which he was buried.

The Church of the Holy Sepulchre in Jerusalem. Thousands of people make special journeys to worship and pray here.

Glossary

Altar The table used for the Eucharist in a Christian church.

Baptism When a Christian is bathed in or sprinkled with water and becomes a member of the Church.

Christianity The religion of people called Christians.

Christians People who follow the religion of Christianity and believe that Jesus Christ is the Son of God.

Church A church is a place where Christians go to worship. Church with a capital "C" means a group of Christians.

Confirmation When a Christian who has been baptized as a baby promises to follow the teachings of Jesus.

Crib A model of the stable where Jesus was born, containing figures, including Jesus, Mary, and Joseph.

Crucifixion How Jesus was killed, by being nailed to a wooden cross.

Disciples The twelve men chosen by Jesus to be his closest followers and friends.

Episcopal Church A group of Christians in the United States who have bishops to lead them.

Eucharist The service at which Christians share bread and wine to remind them of Jesus. The service is also known as Holy Communion, Mass, and the Lord's Supper.

Font A large bowl that holds holy water that is used for baptisms.

Good Friday The day in Holy Week when Christians remember how Jesus was crucified.

Holy Communion See Eucharist.

Holy Week This is the week that leads up to Easter, when Christians remember how Jesus was crucified and then came back to life.

Hymns Songs that praise or thank God.

Icons Pictures of Jesus, Mary, or one of the saints. They are used in worship.

Jesus Christ A Jewish teacher who started Christianity. Christians believe that Jesus was the Son of God. "Christ" was a title given to Jesus by his followers. It means "chosen by God."

Jews An ancient people, many of whom live in Israel.

Minister A man or woman who leads a service in church.

Crib　**Symbol**

Monks and nuns Men and women who have given up ordinary life in order to serve God in special ways.

Nativity The story of Jesus's birth.

Orthodox Church Large groups of Christians who live mostly in Eastern Europe.

Palm Sunday The first day of Holy Week when people waved palm leaves at Jesus as he entered Jerusalem.

Parables Stories with special meanings that Jesus told as part of his teaching.

Paschal candle A special, large candle lit in some churches at Easter to mean that Jesus is alive again.

Pentecostal Church A group of Christians who believe that the Holy Spirit (the power of God) works through them in special ways.

Persecuted When someone is treated very badly because of his or her religious beliefs.

Pilgrims People who make special journeys to holy places.

Prayer Words that are used when talking to God.

Protestant Church A group of Christians who disagreed with the Roman Catholic Church.

Resurrection To rise again from the dead. Christians believe that Jesus rose again after his crucifixion.

Roman Catholic Church The largest group of Christians, led by the Pope who lives in the Vatican in Rome, Italy.

Saint Someone who has led a very holy life and often suffered for his or her religion. After their death, they become saints.

Saint John John was one of Jesus's twelve disciples. He is believed to have written the fourth book of the New Testament.

Sermon A talk given by the vicar, priest, or minister as part of a church service.

Sins Bad actions or words that break religious laws.

Sunday School A place where Christian children learn about God on Sundays.

Symbol An object or sign that has a special meaning and that stands for something else.

Virgin Mary The mother of Jesus.

Index